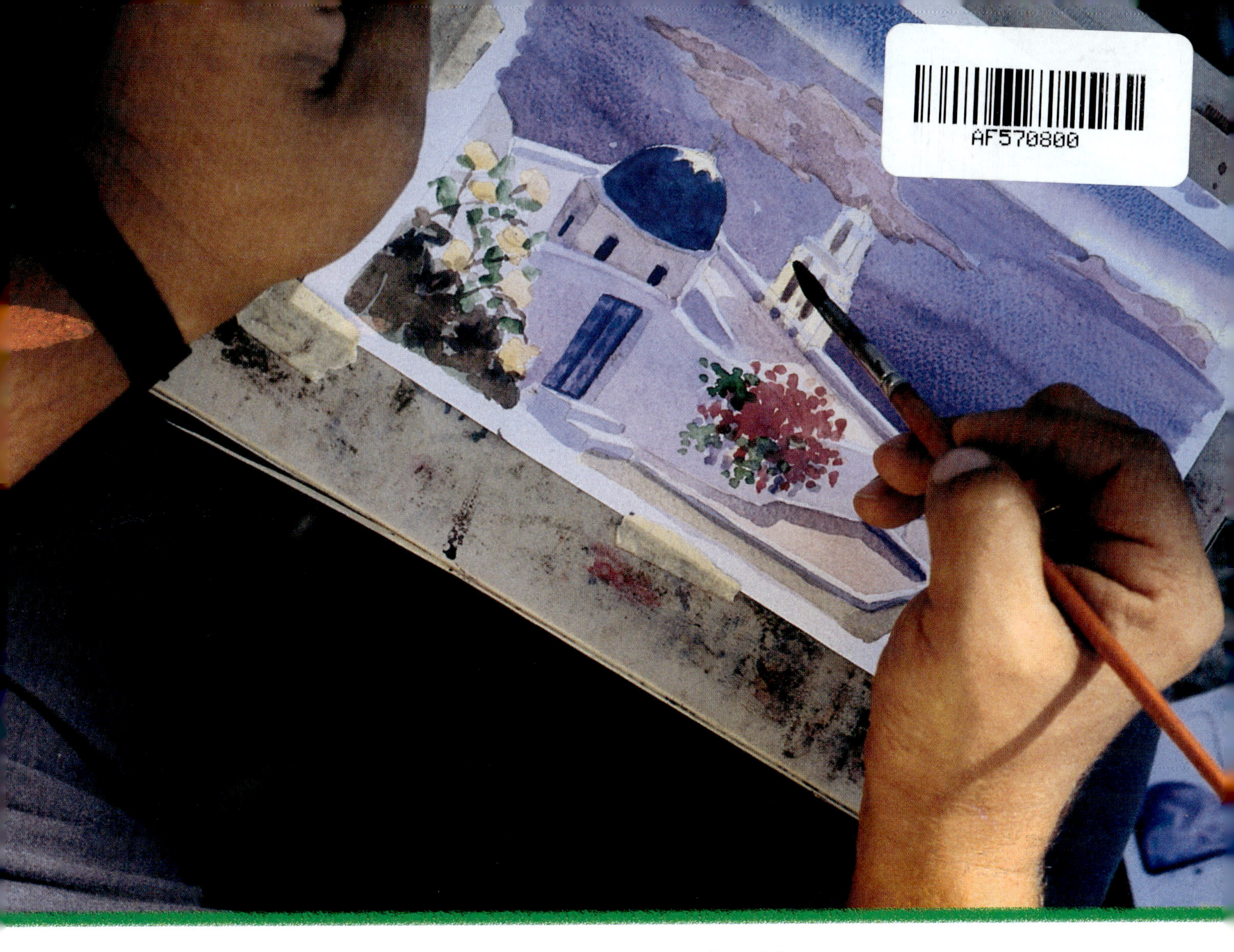

to make a painting.

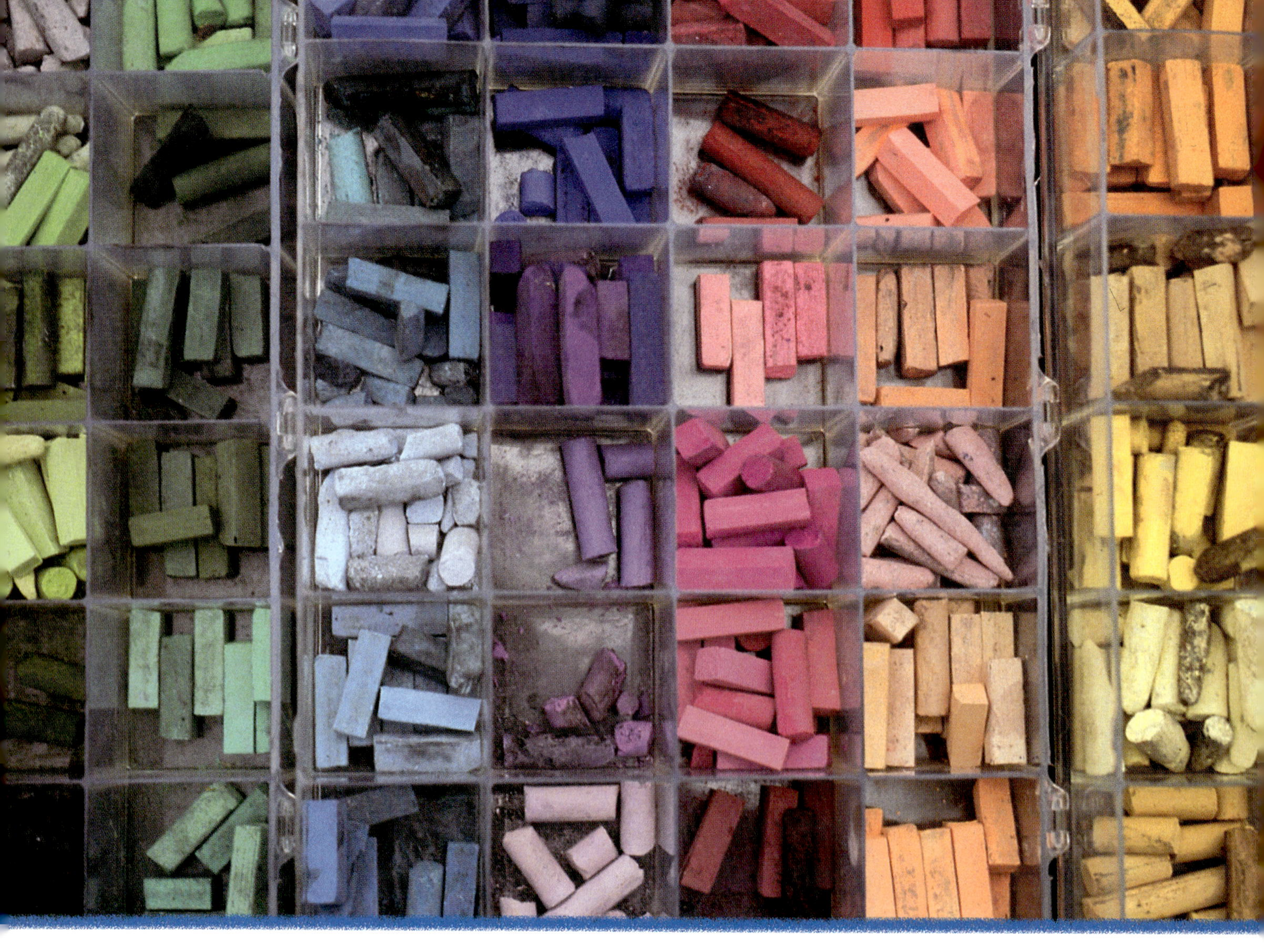

Chalk

WHAT DO ARTISTS USE?

Susan Canizares
Samantha Berger

Scholastic Inc.
New York • Toronto • London • Auckland • Sydney

Acknowledgments

Literacy Specialist: Linda Cornwell

Early Childhood Consultant: Ellen Booth Church

Design: Silver Editions

Photo Research: Silver Editions

Endnotes: Sabrina Jones

Endnote Illustrations: Ruth Flanigan

Photographs: Cover: SuperStock; p1:(tl) Charles Gupton/The Stock Market; (tr) W. Hill, Jr./The Image Works; (bl) David E. Edgerton/Photo Researchers, Inc.; (br) M. Everton/The Image Works; p. 2: SuperStock; p.3: Lyle Leduc/Gamma Liaison; p. 4: M. Everton/The Image Works; p. 5: Philip Bailey/The Stock Market; p. 6: Alan Abramowitz/Tony Stone Images; p. 7: Jeff Greenberg/The Image Works; p. 8: Dan Smetzer/Tony Stone Images; p. 9: Paulo Fridman/Gamma Liaison; p. 10: Jim Steinberg/Photo Researchers, Inc.; p. 11: Linda Bartlett/Photo Researchers, Inc.; p. 12: Pugliano/Gamma Liaison.

Library of Congress Cataloging-in-Publication Data
Canizares, Susan 1960-
What do artists use?/Susan Canizares, Samantha Berger.
p.cm. -- (Learning centers emergent readers)
Sumary: Simple text and photographs introduce the materials artists use to create their work, including paint, chalk, and thread.
ISBN 0-439-04591-6 (pbk.: alk. paper)
1. Artists' materials--Juvenile literature.
[1. Artists' materials.] I. Berger, Samantha. II. Title. III. Series.
N8530.C36 1998
702' .8--dc21 98-53182
CIP AC

3 4 5 6 7 8 9 10 08 03 02 01 00 99

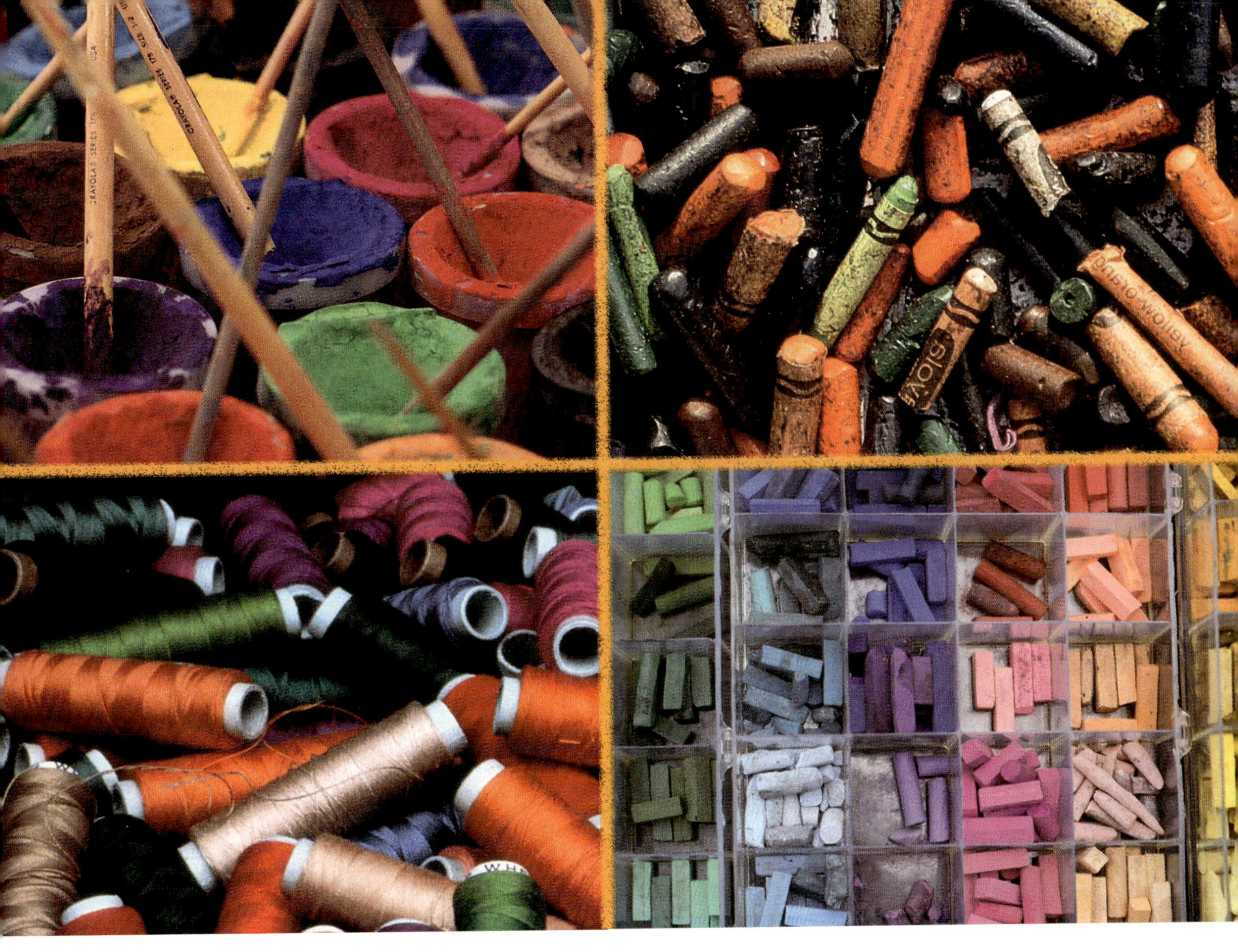

What do artists use?

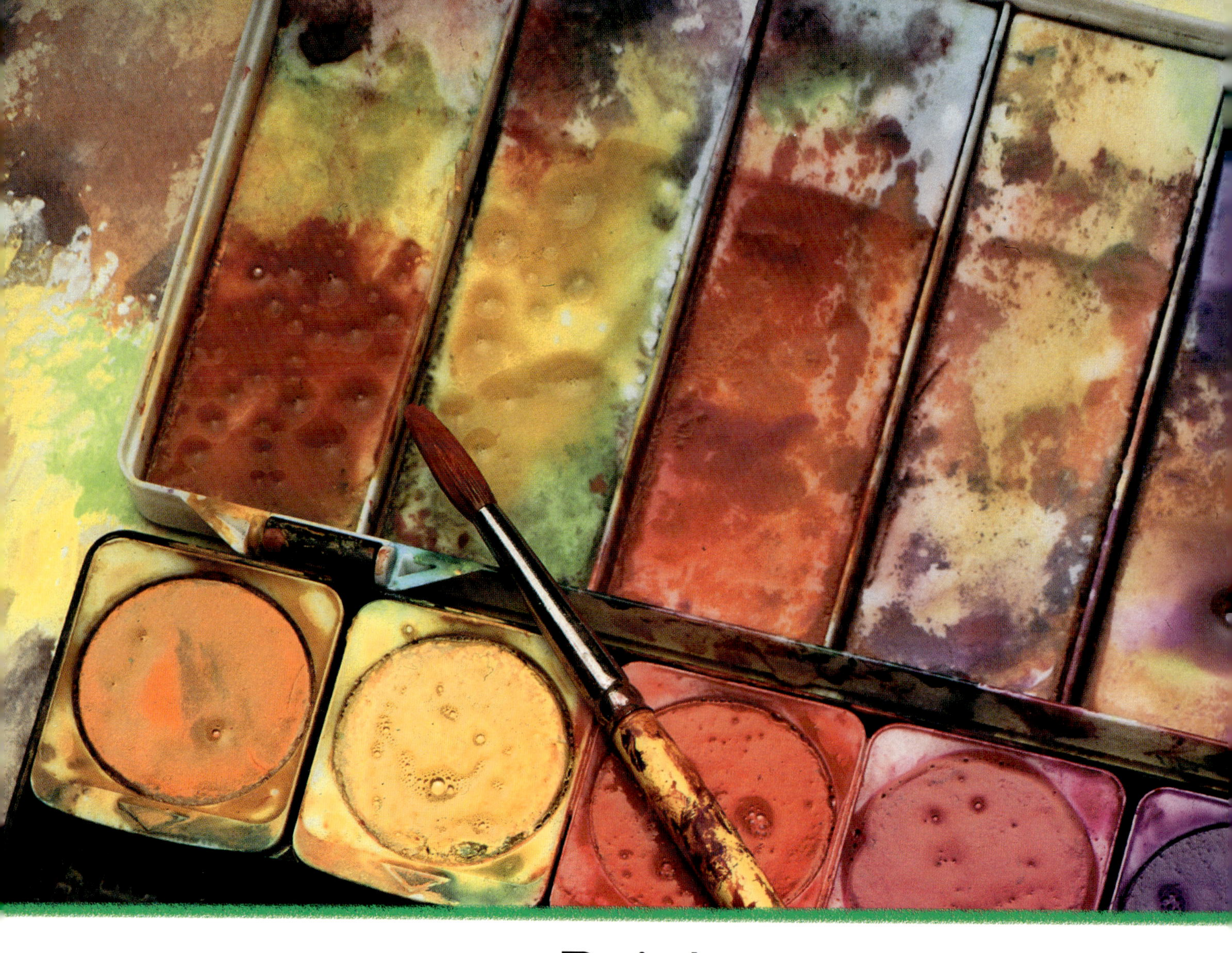

Paint

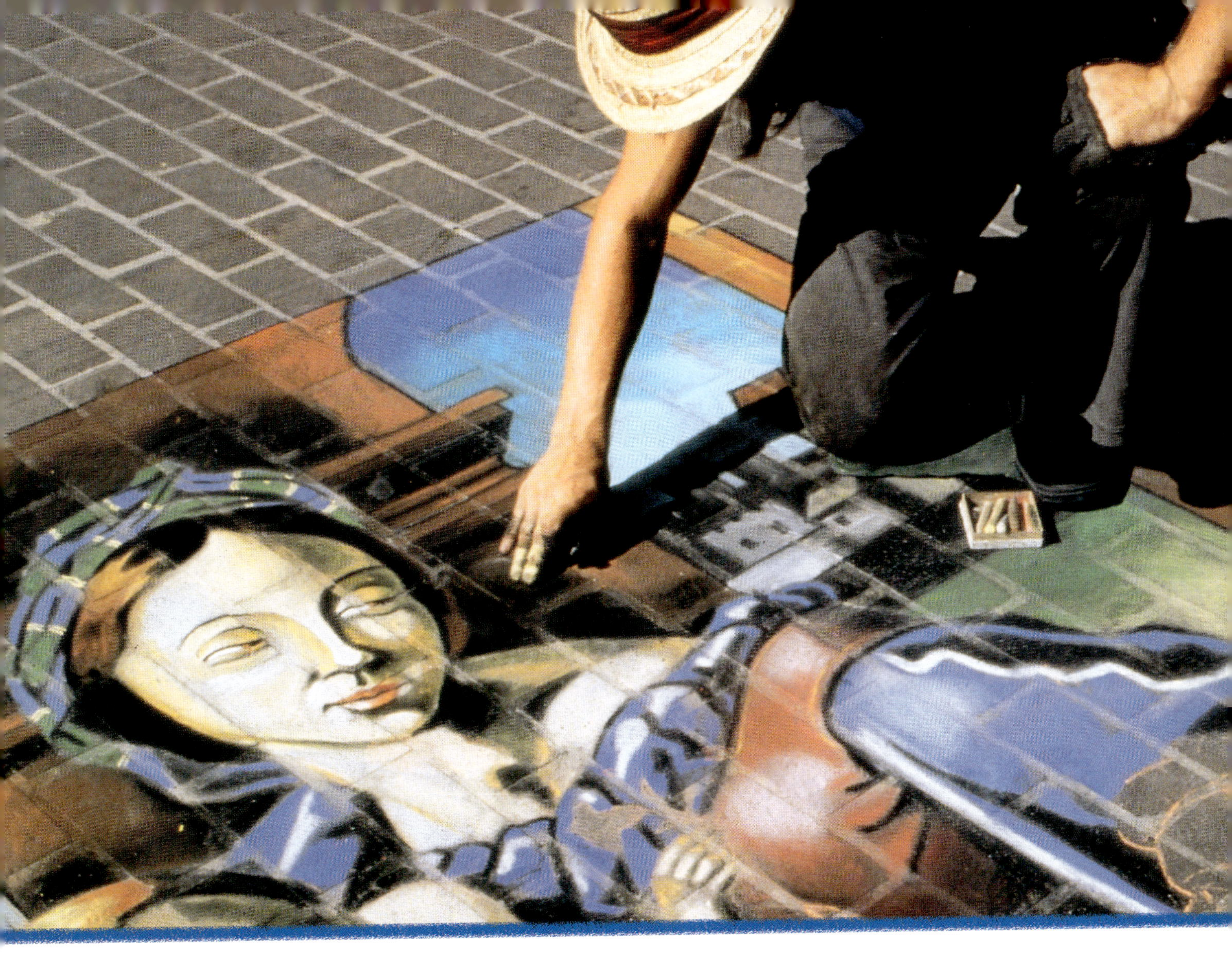

to draw a picture.

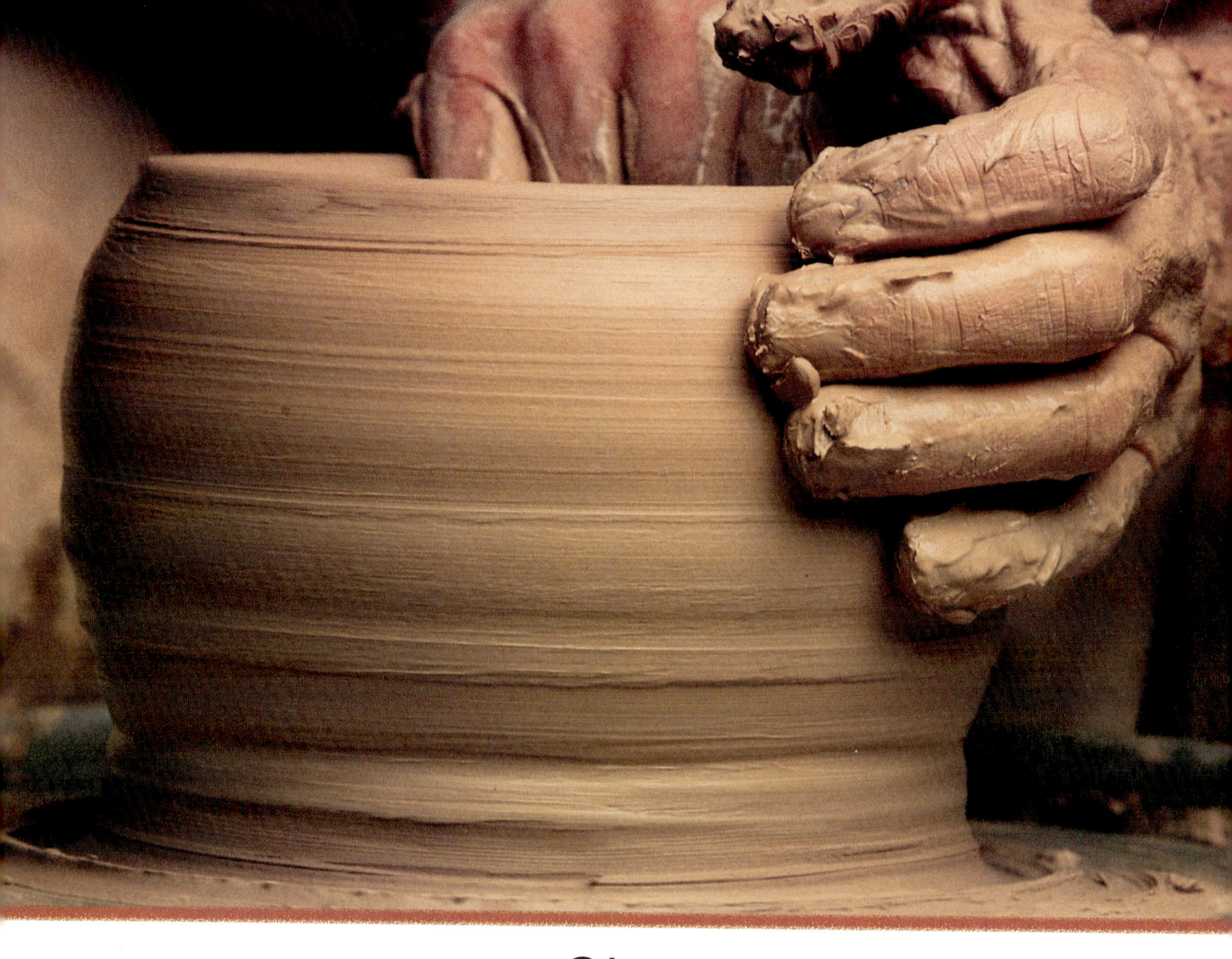

Clay

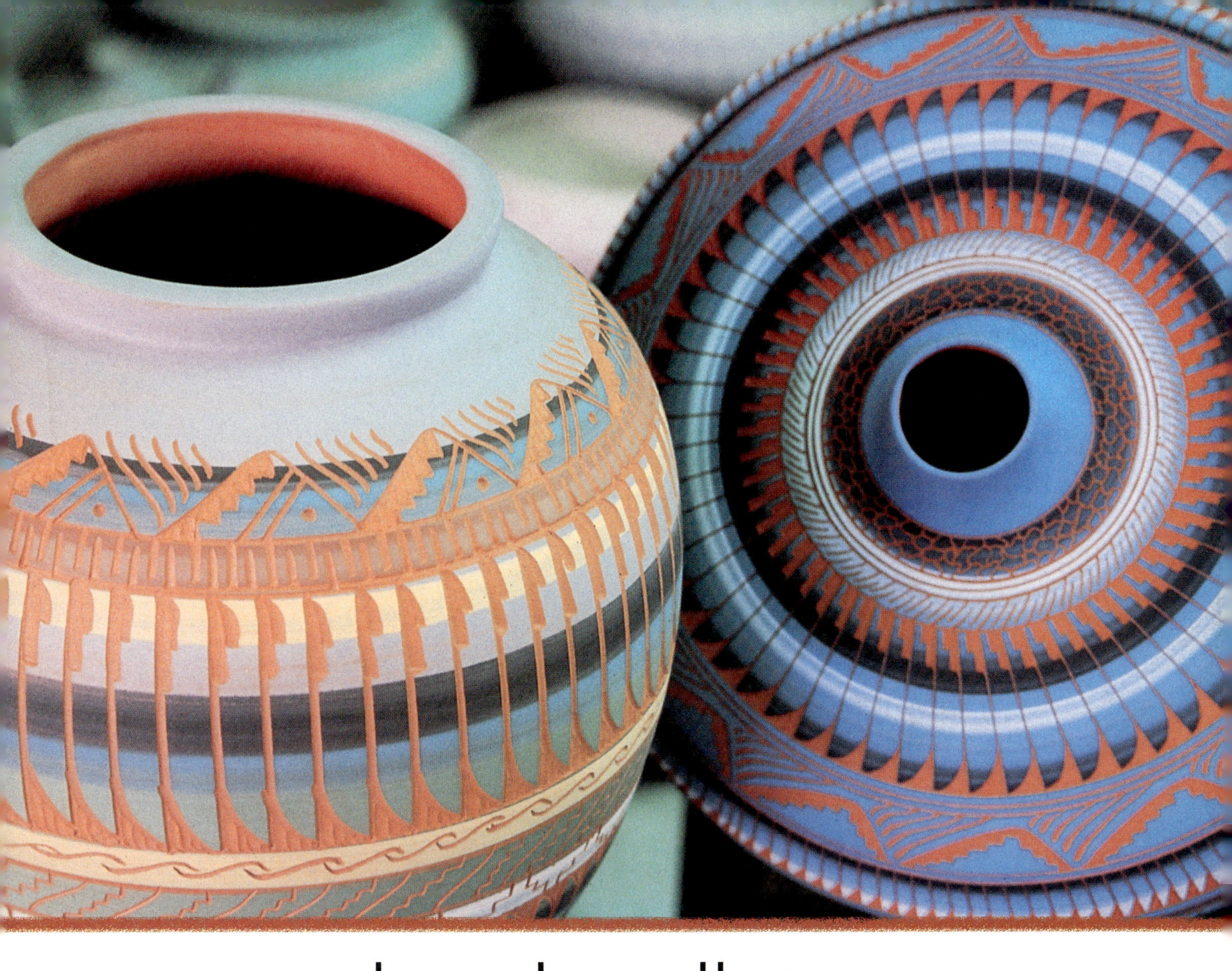

to make pottery.

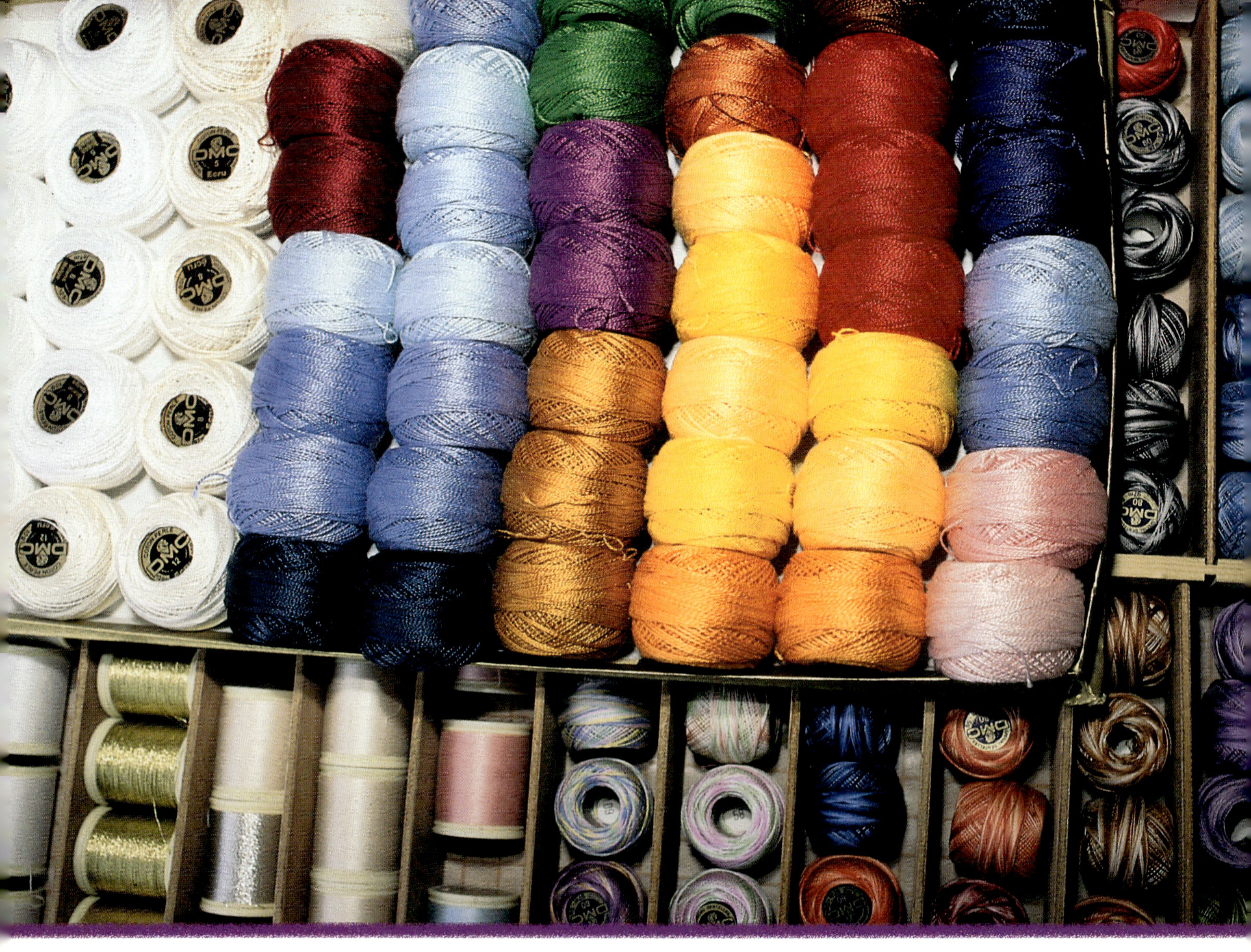

Thread

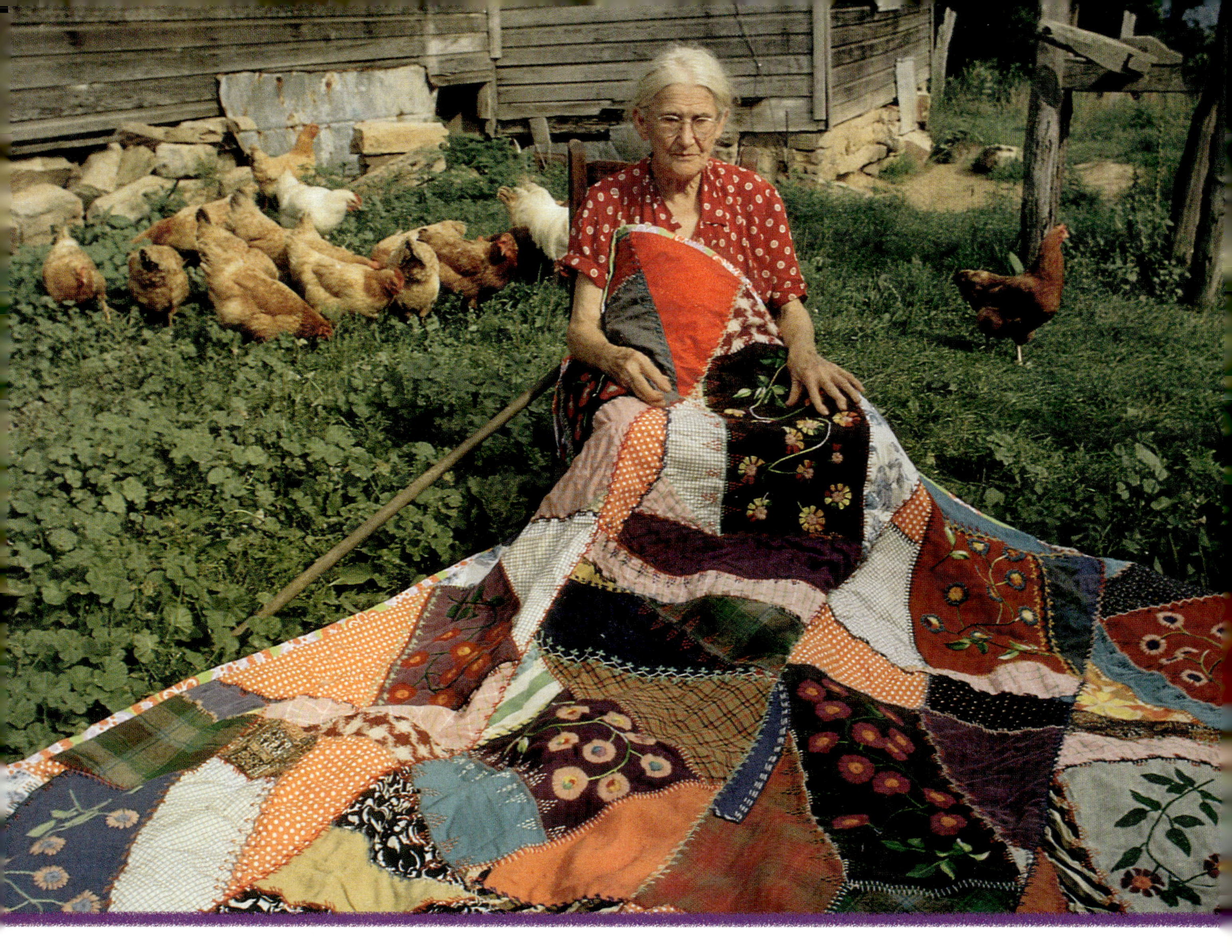

to sew a quilt.

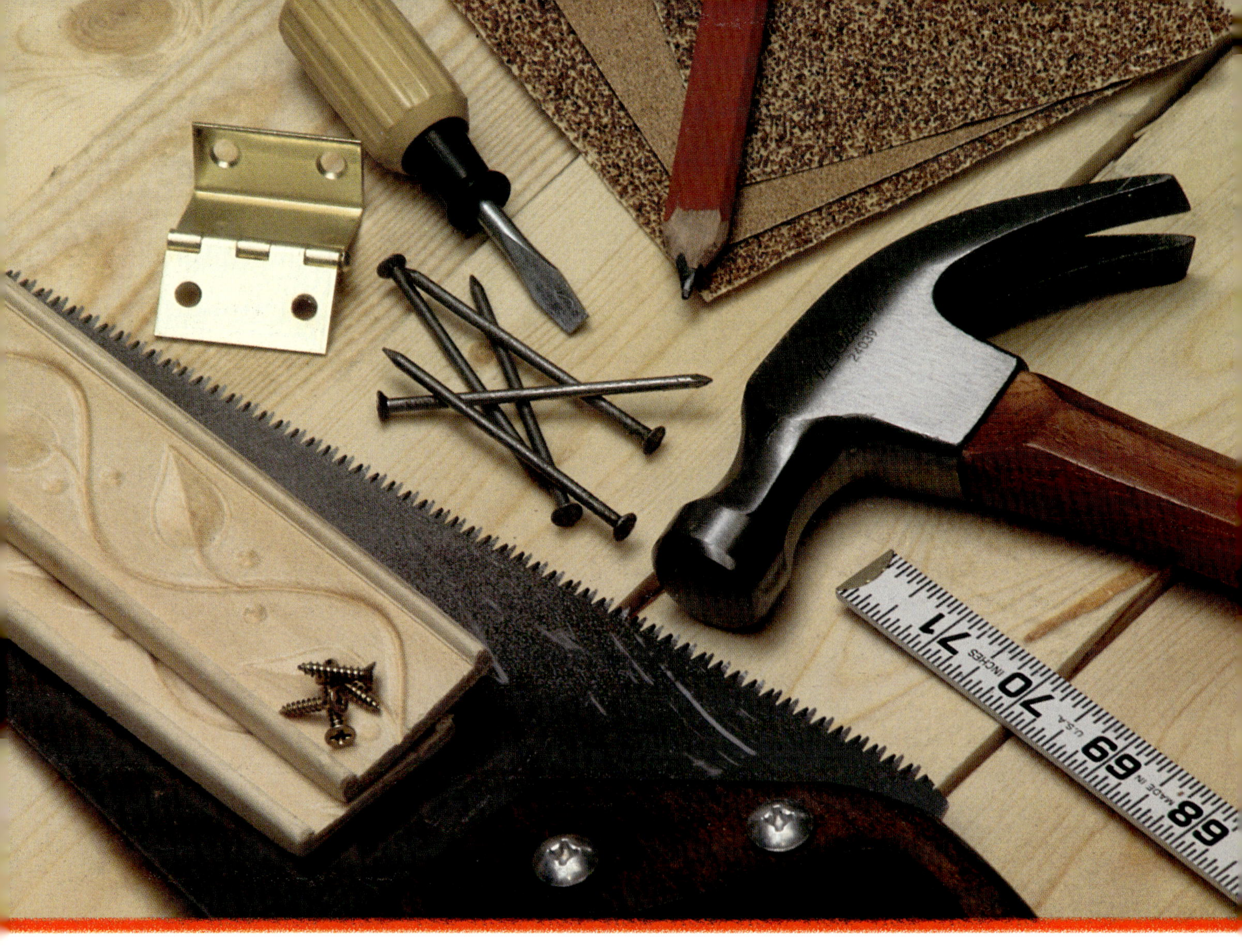

Tools

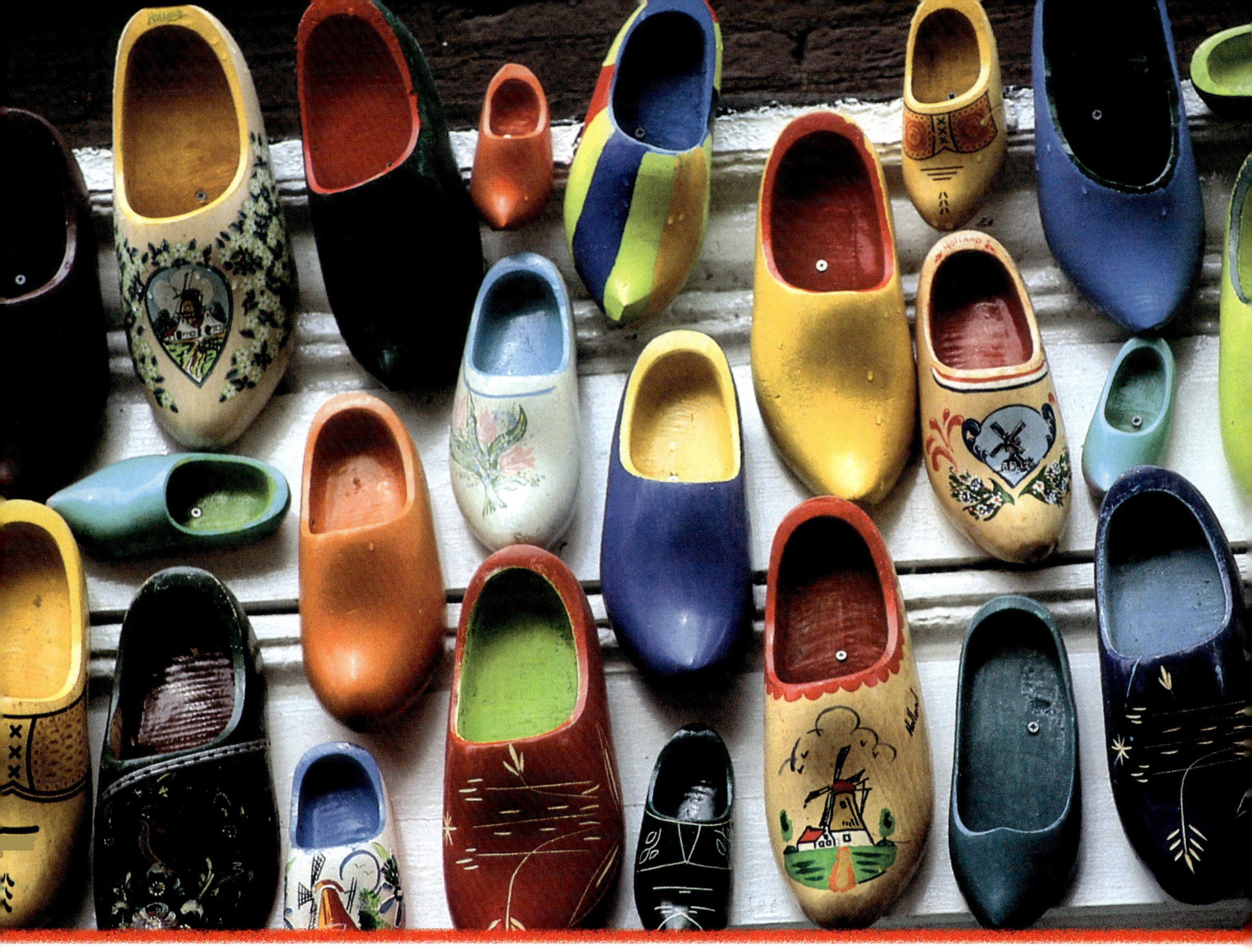

to carve wood.

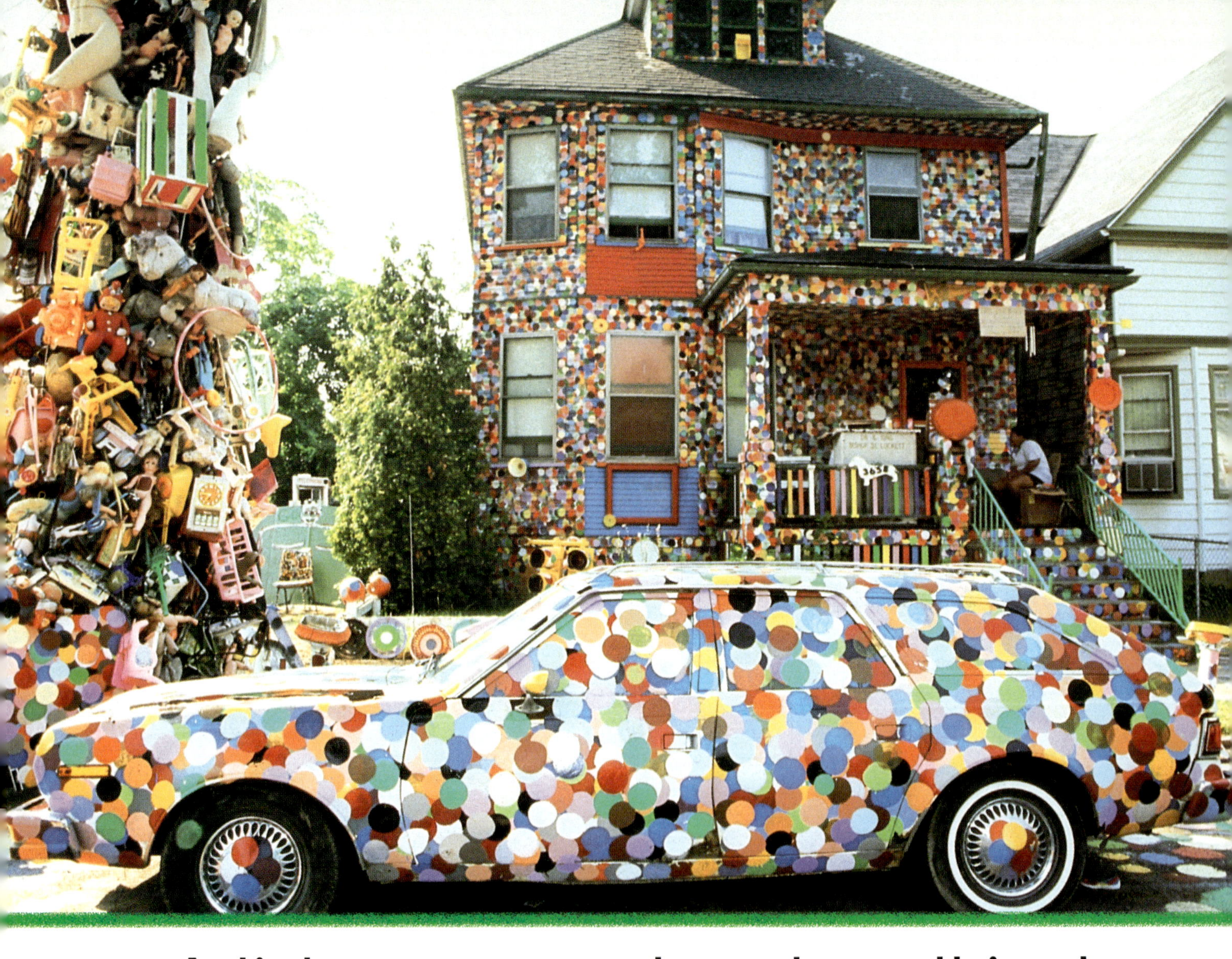

Artists can use almost anything!

WHAT DO ARTISTS USE?

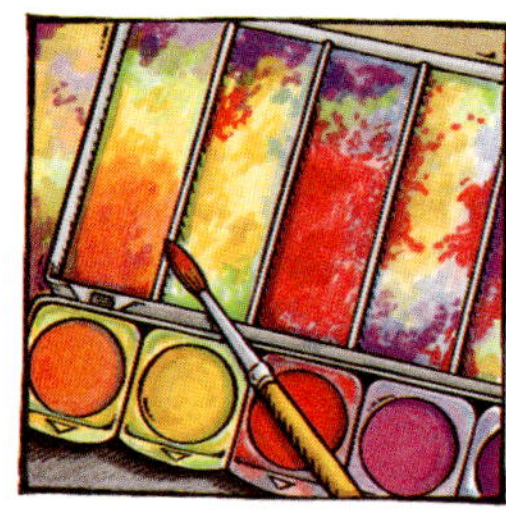

An artist in an art supply store is like a child in a candy store. So many treats, so hard to choose! It would be fun to try them all. Artists choose different materials to make different kinds of art.

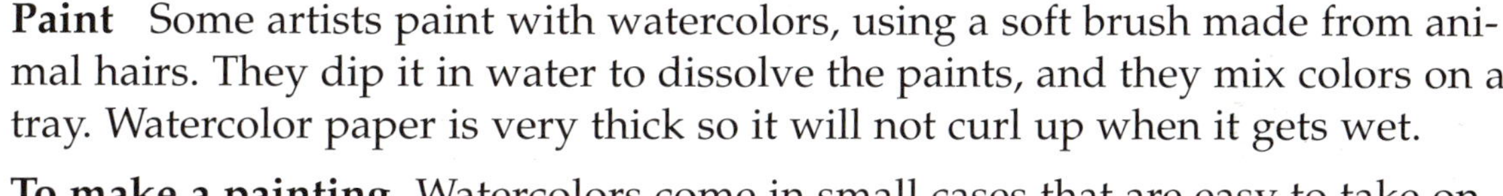

Paint Some artists paint with watercolors, using a soft brush made from animal hairs. They dip it in water to dissolve the paints, and they mix colors on a tray. Watercolor paper is very thick so it will not curl up when it gets wet.

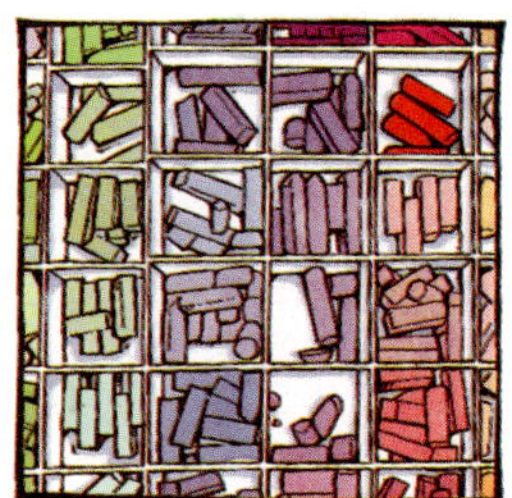

To make a painting Watercolors come in small cases that are easy to take on trips to paint special places. This artist is finishing a painting of a Greek island. The paper is taped onto a board so it will not blow away.

Chalk Powdered pigments are pressed into sticks of chalk that come in all the colors an artist needs. Artists draw with them the same way they do with pencils and charcoal, and then sometimes rub the colors with their fingers to blend them smoothly.

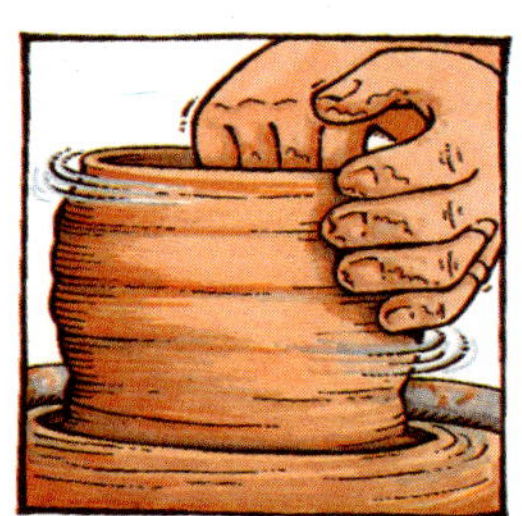

To draw a picture This artist is drawing on the sidewalk, making a very big copy of a painting in a museum. He is blending the background with his fingers. This is in Italy, where there are many famous paintings. People stop to watch him while he is drawing. If they like the picture, they give him a little money, as you would to a musician playing on the street.

Clay Clay comes from the earth. It is dug up from special places in the ground. The artist starts with a lump, which he keeps wet and soft while working on it. To make a round pot, the artist places the lump in the center of a spinning wheel and pulls the sides up with both hands. The artist lets it dry before putting it in a very hot oven called a kiln, to make it hard and waterproof.

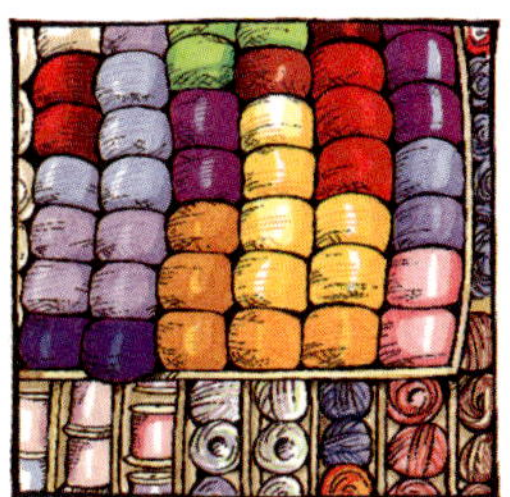

To make pottery Navajo women make this fine pottery the same way their grandmothers and great-grandmothers did. They decorate it with tiny brushes and a steady hand. Indians used to keep food in handmade pots, but these are too delicate to use. They are just to look at.

Thread To make something with this thread, a person would need a needle, scissors, some cloth, and a thimble to protect the finger. Pieces of cloth could be sewn together or decorated with embroidery. There are many different kinds of thread: thick, thin, shiny, fuzzy, and all sorts of colors.

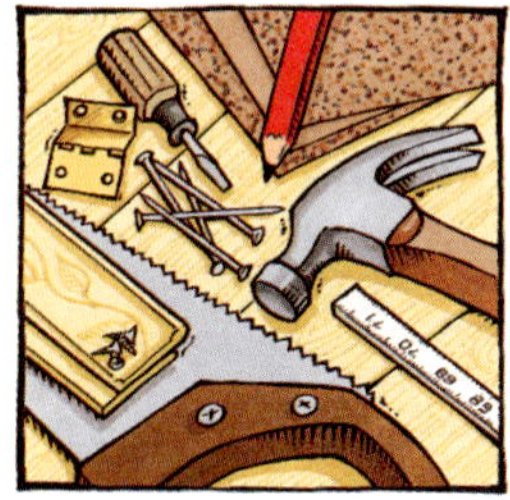

To sew a quilt This woman is showing a patchwork quilt she made out of many kinds of fabric. People make quilts to recycle old clothes or to use up extra material from other sewing projects. This style is called a "crazy quilt" because the patches are in a jumble of mixed-up shapes. Some quilts are made in geometric designs that have been passed on from mother to daughter like a recipe. Others have pictures that tell a story.

Tools These are all tools you would find in a carpenter's or artist's woodworking shop. The artist starts with the pencil and measuring tape, to plan the project. Then he or she might use the saw for cutting and the sandpaper to smooth the wood. The hammer is for pounding nails and the screwdriver is for turning the screws to fasten hinges.

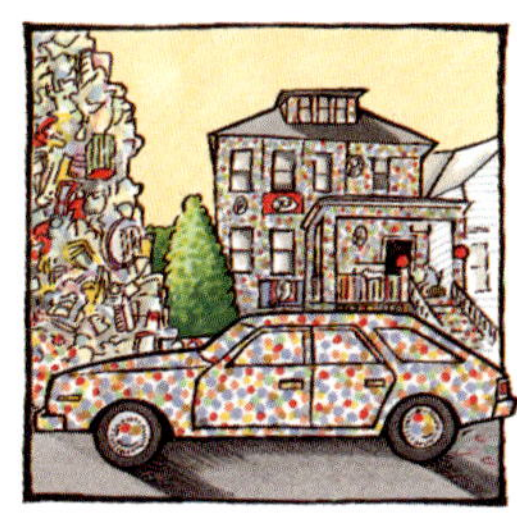

To carve wood These shoes were all carved out of blocks of wood. First the block is fastened to a table with a vise. Then the shape is carved out with a sharp chisel that is tapped with a hammer. A long time ago in rainy Holland, people wore wooden shoes to keep their feet dry while working in the muddy fields on their farms. Now they make these shoes as a beautiful way to show the history of their country.

Almost anything! This artist didn't need to go to the art supply store or the hardware store. The artist found art materials everywhere — even in things you would probably throw out. Art can be made out of old furniture, toys, scraps, even a house or a car! The most important tool any artist can use is his or her imagination.